CAN YOU SPARE A FEW
MINUTES
MAKING MARRIAGE A PRIORITY

HAMP LEE III

(com)**mission**™
PUBLISHING

Recommendations within *Can You Spare a Few Minutes? Making Marriage a Priority* are for informational and educational purposes only. Please consult with the appropriate (and respective) professionals, agencies, or groups before acting on the information in this book.

All scripture references used in this book are from the KING JAMES BIBLE.

Cover photo by Pearl.

Can You Spare a Few Minutes? Making Marriage a Priority/ Hamp Lee III.—3rd ed.

ISBN 978-1-940042-00-8

In loving memory of my Nan and Gramps
...my inspiration for a successful marriage...

CONTENTS

INTRODUCTION

When I met my wife, the only thing I knew about marriage was that I wanted to be like my grandparents. Before my grandfather passed away in 2005, my Nan and Gramps were married for sixty-two years. Though I watched them growing up, I did not understand the depth of the love they shared or the life they built together.

My grandparents spent almost their entire marriage in one house with one phone number. They watched their children, grandchildren, and great-grandchildren grow in front of them. God blessed them with a good life, filled with the fruits of their labor. They were my heroes growing up.

There were so many questions I wish I had asked. I wanted a Nan of my own. I wanted a life-long love to share my days with, but I never asked them what it would take to have a marriage like theirs.

When I asked my girlfriend to marry me nine years earlier, I was ill-prepared to be a husband. I was not mentally, emotionally, financially, or spiritually ready to live with another person. I could barely manage my own life. But there I was, asking one of the most important questions of my life.

Though I knew our marriage was ordained by God, there were many things we could have learned about ourselves before making such an important decision. And because I did not spare a few extra minutes, we found ourselves on the brink of divorce just a few years into our union.

I wrote *Can You Spare a Few Minutes?: Making Marriage a Priority* to share a testimony of God's love and grace through our years of marriage. Since writing this book in 2005, we have recently celebrated our twenty-first year of marriage. I have spent almost my entire adult life with one woman. Through God's help, we have weathered the storms of life and marriage.

There are so many things I wish I could have told that young man kneeling before his girlfriend so many years ago. I learned so many lessons the hard way. But I cannot go back. I can only look to the future and share our experiences with you in the hopes you would avoid some of our mistakes.

No matter where you might be in your marriage, I pray *Can You Spare a Few Minutes?: Making Marriage a Priority* will be a blessing to you and your marriage. As you spare a few minutes to read this book, I pray you will receive a wealth of information to pour into your life and marriage. I pray your marriage before God and others will be a reflection of His love and commitment to us. *Amen.*

1

PRIORITIES

Many marriages suffer or end in divorce because loving God and loving others is not a priority.

When Jesus was asked what was the greatest commandment in the law, He said, *Thou shalt love the Lord thy God with all thy heart, and with all thy soul, and with all thy mind. This is the first and great commandment. And the second is like unto it, Thou shalt love thy neighbour as thyself.*[1]

Loving God should be our chief aim in life, above anything our talents, gifts, or ingenuity can fathom. We should consume ourselves with loving God every day, and in every imaginable way. And because we love Him, we will obey Him.[2]

And as we love God, we will love our neighbors as ourselves. There is no closer neighbor than your spouse. When God is your

---

[1] Matthew 22:37–39.

[2] John 14:15, 15:10; 1 John 5:3.

priority, your spouse sees and experiences the love you have for God and others. But when God is not your priority, you and your spouse might experience hurt, pain, and devastation firsthand.

Over the next several chapters, I will describe what can happen when two people do not make God their priority. You will see my selfish ambition and the pain I caused my wife because I chose not to love her as myself. But you will also see God's love and grace in spite of our own selfishness, disobedience, and sin. You will see what is possible when He gives us a few spare minutes to consider the direction of our lives and to find our way back to Him and His perfect will.

Spare Time

Many marriages suffer or end in divorce because loving God and loving others is not a priority.

Take a few moments to consider this statement and write your thoughts about it.

How has this statement been true or false in your life and marriage?

2

GENESIS

In 1995, I joined the United States Air Force and was assigned to a military base in Japan. Late one Friday night in 1996, I left my dorm room to throw away food I purchased at a restaurant. As I walked in the dayroom, I saw Tonya sitting alone.

After I threw away my trash, I asked her if she was okay and why she was in the dayroom by herself. She said her roommate returned from the base club and brought a guy to their room. She was waiting for him to leave.

Tonya arrived in Japan earlier in the week and did not know anyone. I told her I typically go to the base club on Fridays and a club on an Army post on Saturdays. I told her I was willing to take her to the Army club if she wanted to get out and do something. Since I lived down the hall, I told her to let me know sometime on Saturday.

The next day, I was driving down the street and saw Tonya walking. I asked if she needed a ride. Tonya said she did, but first needed to cash a check at the base club. After we left the club and headed to my car, I was walking in front of her. As I looked back at her, I heard God say, "*This is to be your wife.*"

I had only heard God's voice one other time in my life.[3] Though I was not a Christian and rarely entered a church growing up, I knew it was God speaking to me. Tonya was to be my wife, but I was not ready to be a husband.

After we married, things did not start out as we planned. We argued and fought over many things. We soon learned what *buttons* we could push to make the other person angry, and we pushed them often. It was a revolving cycle of hurt and pain.

In 1997, I went to Alaska for a month-long military trip. While there, one of my co-workers invited me to church several times. Though I did not want to go, I reluctantly agreed.

I will never forget the pastor speaking one weekend on being connected to the power source. I wanted to be connected to the power source. I needed Jesus. My life and marriage were a mess, and I believed at the time, He could help my marriage.

When I called Tonya and told her I wanted to be a Christian, she thought it was a ploy to get her to think differently about me or our relationship. But when I returned home, I started attending church services and was baptized shortly thereafter.

---

[3] When I was about seven years old, I was playing at a neighborhood park. When I looked at a church across the street, I could see through it like having x-ray vision. Though I had never entered into the church, I saw colorful windows along the right wall with long chairs with red covering. There was a man at the front of the church standing on a high stage. He was wearing a gray suit. As he leaned to his left, I heard God say, "*You are to be a preacher.*"

I thought things would get better after I became a Christian. But we actually argued and fought much more. We had an extremely volatile and dangerous relationship. My marriage was not what I expected when I considered having a relationship like my Nan and Gramps. I was spending too much time fighting my wife instead of learning how to love her.

Spare Time

I do not believe anyone wants to have a troubled marriage. We want to live happily with our spouses. We want to experience a life-long love filled with joy and good memories. But somewhere along the way, those desires often become clouded by a reality that seems like a nightmare.

I was a long way from what I saw in my grandparents. Though I found a wife and received favor from the Lord, I failed to see how she was my good thing.[4] I did not know how to turn things around for the better.

Before you continue, I would like for you to take a few moments to consider the following:

Describe how you and your spouse met.

Describe any unresolved issues in your personal lives or relationship (e.g., unforgiveness, previous intimate relationships, significant money problems, etc.)?

---

4 Proverbs 18:22.

Pray about your statements while asking God for his help and intervention.

3

APPEARANCES

As our marriage did not improve, I distanced myself further from Tonya. My church family became an *outlet* from my relationship. They were my source of camaraderie, acknowledgment, and fellowship.

By the next year, I acknowledged my calling to preach the gospel. As the church recognized the gift God placed within me, many church members identified Tonya only as *Hamp's wife*. She hated being called *my wife* instead of Tonya. She did not feel she was considered as her own person and my partner in ministry. I did not see her as a partner in ministry either. The further I embedded myself into the church, the further she drew away.

Tonya wanted the church to be her outlet as well, but my presence there and the reaction of those around us did not make her feel welcome. She felt alone and abandoned by me and the church. Tonya was tired of fighting me and feeling like she was on an island. She had no peace and could not find any comfort.

Because she saw no change in me at home, she could not stand seeing me at church. She saw how I conducted myself in public and how others treated me, while seeing a different person at home. She thought, *If this is what God does for people, I do not want any part of it.*

During the summer of 1999, Tonya wanted to move to another church. She became less interested in our current church's activities and stopped attending. But after everything that happened between us, I thought a move could be an excellent opportunity for us to start over. I could stop serving so actively in the church and focus on us. Maybe this could be the start of a new and better chapter in our lives.

Spare Time

Woe unto you, scribes and Pharisees, hypocrites! for ye are like unto whited sepulchres, which indeed appear beautiful outward, but are within full of dead men's bones, and of all uncleanness. Even so ye also outwardly appear righteous unto men, but within ye are full of hypocrisy and iniquity.—Matthew 23:27–28

Within the church, I was establishing myself as a whited sepulcher. Everyone in the church saw me as righteous outwardly, but my wife knew I was full of hypocrisy and sin. My behavior made church unappealing to her. Though I was being called to preach the gospel to the nations, I could not reach the person closest to me.

How often do we act as if we have everything in our lives together, but in reality, we are completely falling apart? Through social media, business, and beyond we might present an appearance that is not an accurate representation of our lives. Everyone outside of our home sees one side of us and those inside see another.

Have you or your spouse presented yourselves as beautiful outwardly when you had significant issues personally or within your marriage? If so, please describe how your *appearances* affected your marriage.

4

RUNNING

Upon my arrival at the new church, I did not plan on serving in any capacity. But after a few months, I was presented with an opportunity to become the church's youth pastor. I felt I could not pass it up. Though I believed the Holy Spirit was telling me not to accept the position, I accepted the position anyway. I wanted to help the church establish their youth ministry, and I thought the experience I gained at the previous church would be helpful. I ignored my primary reason for transitioning to the church.

Beyond the forty hours I served in the military each week, I served an extra twenty to thirty hours in the church. Many Sundays went by where I sat alone after church—exhausted. The weight of my responsibilities was affecting my mind, body, and emotions.

In November 2000, I was researching youth ministry curriculum to buy for the next year. Instead of spending a large part of our small budget on new curriculum, I came up with a plan to create youth ministry computer disks with teaching lessons, tips, games, and ideas...all before January 1st.

So for the next two months, I spent every free moment I had to complete the project on time. By the last week of December, I finished the last of the computer disks, but I was mentally, emotionally, and physically drained. The added pressure I placed on myself pushed me over the edge.

The Sunday before the New Year, I was up at 2:00 a.m. reviewing my teaching lesson for church. About thirty minutes later, Tonya woke up and asked me when I was coming to bed. Like opening a shaken soda can, I exploded. *What do you mean when am I coming to bed?! I have too much to do, and no one is supporting me. You don't help...*I went on and on.

Tonya did not have any ill-intent in her question. She was only concerned about me because I was staying up so late when I was scheduled to teach in the morning. But I was tired, frustrated, and broken. I was in despair and crying out for help, but I did not know how to properly express myself. So I unleashed my emotions and frustrations on Tonya, an innocent bystander to my poor decisions. I became so enraged that I walked into our bedroom, ripped our footboard off its hinges, and stormed out of the room. Tonya immediately called the military police because, from her point of view, she did not know what I might do next.

I sat quietly in the living room until the military police arrived. When the military police came to our house, they contacted my superiors to determine the appropriate actions to take. One of my superiors asked Tonya if she wanted me to leave. Since Tonya wanted me to leave, I had to pack a bag of clothes and be relocated to a *cool down* room until a course of action could be determined.

Needless to say, I attended church that morning as if nothing was wrong. I did not mention a single word to anyone about what happened a few hours earlier. After the service, I returned to the *cool down* room. About an hour later, my supervisor came to check on me. I opened the door and began explaining the situation to her. The next thing I knew, I was lying on the floor.

When I lifted my head, I felt something wet on my face. I wiped it off with my hand and noticed it was blood. I stood up and stumbled onto the bed, dazed and confused. I turned to the door and noticed it was wide open. It took me a moment to realize I passed out and hit my head on the dresser next to where I was standing. My body finally reacted to the mental, emotional, and physical abuse I subjected it to. A couple minutes later, my supervisor returned with the paramedics to take me to the hospital for further observation.

Spare Time

Have you ever ignored the direction of the Holy Spirit and it affected you and your family? If so, please explain how.

Have you ever been mentally, emotionally, or physically tired and you lashed out at your spouse and/or children? How were they (and your marriage) affected in the short- and long-term?

In prayer, ask God to reveal areas of your life that you might be overcommitted or overworked and if (or where) your marriage has suffered as a result. List any additional areas God identifies and continue to ask Him how you can safeguard the areas of your life that are frayed and worn.

Come unto me, all [ye] that labour and are heavy laden, and I will give you rest. Take my yoke upon you, and learn of me; for I am meek and lowly in heart: and ye shall find rest unto your souls. For my yoke [is] easy, and my burden is light.—Matthew 11:28–30

5

WARNING SIGNS

Where did I go wrong? What could I have done to prevent this?

While in the hospital, God told me this situation was preventable...had I heeded the warning signs. *Warning signs?!* I did not remember seeing any warning signs. And if I had seen them, I figured I would have paid more attention to them. But I did receive two warnings from God:

1999

In the first few months of accepting the youth pastor position, I wanted to resign. My workload at home and work was too much to bear. I could not find a balance between my personal life, family, work, and the church. Though I spoke to my pastor about my concerns, I did not resign.

2000

A few months into the year, God told me to read 1 Timothy 3:5:

For if a man know not how to rule his own house, how shall he take care of the church of God?

The conviction of this scripture hit me hard. My household was a mess. There was no peace and little love in our home. I could see it in my daughter's eyes. There was no way I was taking care of my household in a manner that would please God. I wanted to resign right away.

But I ignored God's warnings. I felt the work I was doing for God was of greater importance. And in the end, I paid a hefty price: a broken home and a night's stay in the hospital.

After being discharged from the hospital, I continued serving in the youth ministry. Though God was chastising me out of love,[5] I did not respond. *What was it going to take to get my attention?*

Spare Time

Like a loving parent, God warns us of impending danger. Words of correction, conviction, and counsel from God are meant to keep us safe in His will.

Describe a situation where you received convictions to change or adjust an area of your life and/or marriage and you did not heed God's warnings. How was your life and/or marriage affected as a result?

---

5 Hebrews 12:5–6.

6

THE
WILDERNESS

Life at home was terrible. Tonya and I fought and argued on a daily basis. We could barely hold a decent conversation. The constant fighting made me feel lonely, unsupported, and unloved. Things were so bad between us that I was willing to live in the wilderness than spend another day in the house with her.[6] But I soon learned that when you live in the *wilderness*, you expose yourself to the perils of the environment around you.

A few months later, I started talking to a young woman from the church. We did not talk about anything sexual or inappropriate. Our conversations often focused on God, church, and college work. Everything was very harmless. It felt good to talk

---

[6] Proverbs 21:19.

to a woman without arguing all the time. It was like a breath of fresh air.

As the days went on, this young woman and I laughed, cried, and prayed together. What I should have been looking for in Tonya, I was desperately searching for in this other woman. There were even times when I would argue with Tonya just so I would have a reason to talk with this other woman.

I was not paying attention to the direction of my heart or emotions. This woman was feeding an emotional void in my life, and I felt my heart and body wanting to draw closer to her. It seemed like an *automatic response* to all she had been giving me in time and conversation. This was when I recognized the line of infidelity drawing dangerously close.

By God's grace, Tonya confronted me about this relationship a few days later. She saw what was going on and read the warning signs a lot better than I wanted to act on them. And to expose my inappropriate behavior and flawed character, she contacted the pastor.

The pastor quickly asked us to come to his house to talk about Tonya's recent confession. Our meeting with the pastor defused some of the tension between us and dissolved the friendship I had with the other woman. But there were many other issues that remained beneath the surface.

Spare Time

When we are arguing, fighting, and hurting emotionally, we might seek external outlets for relief. Some outlets are healthy, but others lead down paths of pain and destruction. But even when we know certain outlets are potentially dangerous or destructive, some might not care because they will do whatever is necessary to find *peace, happiness, and relief*. This is an extremely dangerous position to take as there are significant long-term and eternal implications.[7]

When you are feeling frustrated, burned out, or emotionally drained, what outlets do you use to find *peace, happiness, and relief*? Would God approve of the places, people, and conversations you are having? Why or why not?

Have you ever ignored the dangers of a particular person, place, or thing because of your desires for *peace, happiness, and relief*? If so, please explain.

Why should you be cautious of the people, places, and things you seek for counseling and support? How can they cause additional problems for you and your marriage?

Describe at least three safe outlets you can use for counseling, help, and support.

Ponder the path of thy feet, and let all thy ways be established. Turn not to the right hand nor to the left: remove thy foot from evil. —Proverbs 4:26

---

[7] Proverbs 5:1–13; Galatians 5:19–21; Revelation 21:8.

7

CONQUERED

My end was near. I could feel it.

In May 2001, I talked to the pastor about resigning after the summer. I had made a lot of bad decisions in my marriage, and I was hoping it was not too late to salvage it. But at the same time, Tonya had reached her wit's end. She decided to leave Japan and our marriage for good.

I was not surprised by her decision to leave. Instead of building her up, I tore her down. I trampled on her love and spit on her well-being. The fruit from my life produced nothing but pain and heartache into hers.

When I spoke with one of our church elders about Tonya's decision, he told me that if I did not pay attention to her and focus on her needs before she left, she was not going to return. So for the few weeks prior to her departure, I tried following through on his counsel. But it was hard to focus on her needs when I had issues as well.

At first, I was hurt and sad because she was leaving, and then I became angry. I just wanted her to leave as fast as possible and leave me alone. I wanted it over!

My anger was a way of deflecting the hurt and pain I had in my heart. I did not have a better or more mature way to express myself. I hurt a lot of people and failed in so many areas of my life. I wished I could have hidden somewhere far, far away.

A few weeks later, I contacted the pastor and told him that under the current circumstances in my life, I was immediately resigning as the youth pastor. Though I had commitments for the youth ministry throughout the summer, I did not have the will to continue any longer.

The pastor asked me to come to his house a couple days later to talk about my resignation. He told me that along with resigning as the youth pastor, I could sit out from my duties as a minister and sit on the front row to be ministered to. I told him that in addition to resigning, I would not be attending his church any longer. It would have been too embarrassing for me to look at the people I failed. When he asked me if I had prayed about my decision, I told him no.

Spare Time

Pride goeth before destruction, and an haughty spirit before a fall.—Proverbs 16:18

Pride.

Looking over the past several chapters, pride was an underlying theme in my life. I was so focused on what I wanted that I allowed my pride to blind me from the path of destruction. Even when God and my wife tried to step in to intervene, I would not heed their warnings. I only saw what I wanted.

Have you experienced the destruction of various areas of your life and marriage due to pride? If so, please explain. Have others tried to warn you about your conduct? Did you heed their advice? Why or why not?

What decisions have you made to bring your marriage to the state it is in today? Do not include the actions of your spouse.

8

INTERMISSION

After Tonya and my daughter left Japan, we argued almost every day. I kept telling her she was coming back, while she was determined to find employment and start a new life without me.

Each day, I felt empty and defeated. I was alone in an empty house, with no one to talk to, and no inner peace. The two most precious people in my life were gone.

But if they were so precious to me, why did I not I act like they were when they were here?

Why did I not heed the warnings?

Why was I so wrapped up in myself?

By the end of the summer, Tonya called me and said she was returning. Although I wanted her to return, I was a little shocked by her decision because we were arguing so much.

One evening before Tonya returned, I was walking around the military base to reflect and pray. Before my walk ended, God told me to separate myself from the church.

Separate from church?! What about Hebrews 10:25?

During my separation, God told me to do three things:

1. Speak to myself...because what was in me would be enough to sustain me. (At the time, I did not realize God was speaking of the Holy Spirit.)

2. Seek the fellowship of one person.

3. Fellowship with one group.

God explained that through these three things, I would fulfill Hebrews 10:25. Though I did not understand the reason for leaving the church or know where this would lead, I wanted to be obedient and trust His leading.

Everything I knew to be true about the church would change. I did not know what people would say or how they would react. Although I was filled with uncertainty, I settled in my heart to say yes to God. In spite of all I had done against Him, His Name, and my family, God never left me or forsook me...His grace was truly sufficient.

Spare Time

Within our lives, there are times when we need to take an intermission. We need opportunities to reflect, reset, and restore. Whether we have the luxury of a getaway weekend, a few hours to drive on the highway, or the ability to take a long walk, there are significant benefits in having an intermission. Sometimes we need moments to quiet our minds, calm our souls, and keep our bodies still. Intermissions allow God an opportunity to capture our attention and lead us where we need to be—within His perfect will.

Within the next couple weeks, I would like for you to take one or more intermissions. Spend time sitting at your favorite spot on the beach, driving on the highway, sitting quietly at church, or finding a solitary place where you can hear the gentle whispers of a loving Father. Spend time enjoying the beauty of God's creation and speak as little as possible. Pray and meditate. Write down your experiences.

9

BELIEVE

For as he thinketh in his heart, so is he... —Proverbs 23:7a

Because of the state of our marriage, it was hard for me to believe any positive change was possible. Though every day of our marriage was not bad, it seemed as if the negative days overshadowed the good ones.

As my thoughts on our marriage were mostly negative, my actions soon followed. I started looking for scriptures on divorce and responding negatively to Tonya. I would do and say things that did not align with someone wanting to remain married. But God wanted me to understand that I could not continue thinking negatively about Tonya or our marriage. Instead of searching for scriptures about divorce, I had to find scriptures on how to build our marriage. I had to believe our marriage could be restored, regardless of what we had been through or what I saw in front of me.[8] I had to overcome my overwhelming feelings of hopelessness. I had to believe.

Spare Time

A father brought his son to Jesus' disciples to be delivered from a dumb spirit that tormented him. But the disciples were not able to cast the spirit out.[9] There was a large crowd around them and the scribes started arguing with the disciples over the matter. When Jesus came to them, He asked what they were arguing about. The father spoke out about his son and what the disciples were unable to do. [10]

As a father, he had a responsibility to care for his child—to provide, protect, and prepare. But his son was possessed by a spirit that took over his body from childhood. The spirit caused him to be torn, foam at the mouth, and grind his teeth. This had to be hard to watch and dangerous for both the father and those around the boy. But the father did not give up.

Though he could not do anything for his son, he took him to those he thought could help. But when the disciples were unable to help, the father did not leave. He stayed as the scribes argued with the disciples. When Jesus asked about their argument, he spoke up for his son.

---

[8] 2 Corinthians 5:7.

[9] Mark 9:17–24.

[10] Mark 9:14–16.

Now, I cannot speak for the father, but based on what is provided in Mark 9:17–24, he might have been unsure of what Jesus could do. After seeing his son go through so much suffering and knowing the disciples who walked with Jesus could not help, his belief might have been shaken. So the father cried out with tears, *Lord, I believe; help my unbelief.*[11]

Many of us today might find ourselves in the same position as the father. At the beginning of our marriage, we were filled with hope, love, and joy. But somewhere along the way, things changed. The person we fell in love with changed. Maybe we changed. The beautiful marriage we pictured with our spouse becomes a mirage, a shadow of what could have been as we face the bitter pain of an unwelcome reality. And this reality might have shaken our belief that things will get better. We struggle to believe our marriage will ever change.

But the father knew exactly where to go to seek help for his son. Jesus was not around,[12] but he came to His disciples for help. He did not give up. He was committed to his son. There was a seed of belief. And when the father came to Jesus, he explained that he believed, but asked for help in his unbelief.

When things do not go as we planned—whether in marriage or life—we must go to the One we know who can help us. We can go to God whether we believe a little or not at all. And as we come to

---

[11] Mark 9:24.

[12] Mark 9:2–13.

Him, He can reignite our faith to help us face and overcome the challenges before us.[13]

Describe a time when you might have doubted your marriage could survive trying times.

How difficult has it been for you—now or in the past—to believe your marriage could be better?

When you have been frustrated or angry about your marriage, have you searched for scriptures on divorce or talked with someone you knew would agree with your negative views? Please explain. How could this be unhealthy?

Have the circumstances in your marriage affected your views about God? If so, please explain how.

What can you do today to begin a change in your beliefs (Matthew 11:28–30; Revelation 2:1–7)?

---

[13] Isaiah 40:30–31.

10

THE ART OF
MARITAL WARFARE

The Philistines gathered their armies for battle against Israel.[14] They each drew battle lines on two mountains facing one another with a valley between them.

From out of the Philistines' camp came a champion named Goliath. He stood over nine feet tall.[15] He had a bronze helmet and wore scale-armor that weighed one hundred twenty-five pounds. Goliath also wore leg armor made of bronze and carried a bronze javelin on his shoulder. He was prepared for battle.

---

[14] I Samuel 17.

[15] I Samuel 17:4.

Goliath shouted to have a man from Israel fight him. But the king and all of Israel were distressed and greatly afraid.[16] Goliath did this for forty days.

One day, a young man named David came into Israel's camp and heard Goliath shouting to Israel. He asked the men who stood by him, *What shall be done to the man that killeth this Philistine, and taketh away the reproach from Israel? for who is this uncircumcised Philistine, that he should defy the armies of the living God?*[17]

A short while later, the king learned what David said, and he asked to see him. When David came before the king, he said, *Let no man's heart fail because of him; thy servant will go and fight with this Philistine.*[18] The king noticed that David was only a youth. He said he could not fight against the Philistine. But David described how he used to keep sheep for his father. When a lion or bear came and took a lamb from the flock, he went after them, struck them, and delivered the lamb from their mouth. And if they rose up against him, he caught them by their beard, struck them, and killed them. As David killed both lions and bears, he knew Goliath would face the same fate, for he defied the armies of the living God.[19] *The Lord that delivered me out of the paw of the lion, and out of the paw of the bear, he will deliver me out of the hand of this*

---

[16] 1 Samuel 17:8–11.

[17] 1 Samuel 17:24–27.

[18] 1 Samuel 17:32.

[19] 1 Samuel 17:33–36.

Philistine. In response, the king said, *Go, and the Lord be with thee.*[20]

When the king placed his armor on David and gave him a sword, David said he could not go out with these. He had not tested them. So David went out to meet Goliath with what he was familiar with: his staff, a sling, and five smooth stones.[21]

War is never pretty. Each side will often do whatever they can, using whatever they have (and are familiar with) to win. Unnecessary pain, suffering, destruction, or death become collateral events toward their goal to overcome and conquer.

When it came to my marriage, things started out good for the first few months. But it did not take long before we drew battle lines. We fought one another for control of the marriage.

We wanted the marriage to be run the way we wanted. We wanted to be the boss of the other person. There was absolutely no room for compromise until the other person surrendered to our will. Neither of us was willing to back down. We fought for complete domination. Peace was only an option if it was in our favor.

As we fought for control, we knew exactly what *buttons* to push to make the other person upset. If she said something that upset me, I would push her buttons to upset her. Most of the time, I did not mean what I was saying or doing, but in the heat of the moment, all I could think about was winning the battle. I did not care what words I used or how they affected her. I wanted to *win* at

---

[20] 1 Samuel 17:37.

[21] 1 Samuel 17:38–40.

all costs. But I did not understand how our warfare was changing us and our marriage.

With each sharp word and action, we were cutting one another. There might not have been physical scars or bruises, but our minds, hearts, and souls were being deeply wounded. We were suffering from the pain of our words and actions. But all we saw was an enemy standing in front of us.

It took me a long time to understand that my wife was not my enemy. She was not the person I should be looking to battle every day. God joined us together as one flesh, for a specific purpose for His glory. We should help one another stand against the wiles of the devil,[22] bear one another's burdens,[23] and help each other accomplish the work God gave us.

When a husband and wife fight one another, they entangle themselves in the affairs of this life.[24] They become unable to focus on the purpose and assignment they were given from God. They spend their days fighting one another rather than loving God, loving one another, and carrying out their mission.

Spare Time

If you and your spouse *war* with one another, describe some of the issues you have fought over? What weapons have you used against him or her (e.g., words, actions, etc.)?

What have you gained from warring with your spouse?

---

[22] Ephesians 6:11.

[23] Galatians 6:2.

[24] 2 Timothy 2:4.

Describe the task, purpose, or mission given to your family. Has your *warring* affected your ability to accomplish your task, purpose, or mission? If so, please explain how.

Read James 4:1–10. How can you relate to these verses? What can you do to make peace with God and your spouse?[25]

_____

25 Matthew 5:9.

11

GOING OUT
OF BUSINESS

Seeing a business close its doors for the last time was often a sad sight for me. That business was once a fulfilled dream. The owner had expectations and goals. Owning a business might have been one of the happiest and proudest moments in their lives. It could have provided the hope of independence and financial prosperity. But now, the business that provided so much hope and promise was no more.

I often wondered how these business owners felt. Sure, there might be disappointment, as no one wants to come to a decision to close their business, but maybe the closure provided an even greater opportunity in the future. Maybe their experience taught them very valuable lessons, giving them even greater hope for their next venture. Sometimes, experience becomes a teacher. And this is what I hoped for my marriage.

Before Tonya and I married, I was hoping to have a marriage that lasted a lifetime. I assumed I would have a happy wife and a happy life. But as time went on, my marriage was far from this ideal.

Our marriage was being devastated from our many arguments and fights. We were almost *out of business*. But God was giving us another opportunity to keep the doors of our marriage open. And if our marriage was going to improve, our flesh (old ways, sin nature) had to go *out of business*.[26] We had to change how we conducted ourselves to see any improvement in our relationship.

If I wanted to experience a better marriage, I could not expect it just because I wanted it. Wanting change and seeing change are two separate issues. I would need to act different to receive a different result. What I believed and how I acted had to line up.

Spare Time

Many of us keep our flesh *in business* because it is convenient and comfortable. We spent a lifetime learning how to conduct *business* our way. It is how we grew up and what we know. We follow God when things are good, but as soon as trials or tribulations arise, we might turn away from Him.[27]

Our flesh cannot remain in business. Through Christ, we can find the encouragement, strength, and ability to become the person He

---

[26] Colossians 3:9–13.

[27] Matthew 13:20–21.

desires us to be.[28] We can shut the doors of our flesh and open a *business* of happiness, peace, and joy in the Holy Spirit.[29]

Are there areas of your life that might need to go *out of business*? If so, please describe.

How has your dependence on your flesh affected your marriage?

Meditate on the following scriptures: Joshua 1:1–9; Psalm 1, 119:1–16; Proverbs 3:1–8; Hebrews 12:1–3. In what ways can you go *out of business*?

---

[28] Romans 8:27–29; 2 Corinthians 12:8–10; Galatians 6:9–10; Philippians 4:13.

[29] Romans 14:17.

12

TRAFFIC COP

A traffic cop is one who directs traffic in areas where there are little or no controls for motor vehicles. He or she is placed in a myriad of situations to evaluate and diffuse any traffic congestion. The traffic cop can use any sequence of commands as he or she sees fit to establish an orderly and safe flow of traffic. People under the guidance of the traffic cop are required to respond to his or her commands or face negative repercussions.

The Holy Spirit had sought to relieve the congested areas of my life and marriage, but I failed to heed His directions; I chose my own way. Because of this, I placed my marriage on the road toward divorce. Now, I may not understand why God asks something of me, like being separated from the church, but He speaks and acts in totally separate ways from my own.[30]

---

[30] Isaiah 55:8–9.

There will be times when the Holy Spirit will quicken me to speak. Then there are other times when I need to listen to Tonya without saying a word, when I may want to give her a *piece* of my mind...or I need to hold her, console her, encourage her, or correct her (in love). I will have to listen to His still, small voice motioning me toward the Father's will. It is in these opportunities that I must say, *not my will, but Your will be done.*

Spare Time

The Holy Spirit has been sent as a counselor to guide us into all truth.[31] Even if you may think you know what you are doing, your plans are fallible and can push you outside of God's will.[32] But through obedience to God's word and voice, you will receive all you need to love your spouse the way He intends.

Make a commitment to following the Holy Spirit. The Holy Spirit is no respecter of persons and He is not a people-pleaser. He will work to help you live within God's perfect will.

How has the Holy Spirit been (or tried to be) a counselor in your life and marriage?

What guidance have you received from the Holy Spirit concerning your marriage? Have you been obedient to His leading? Why or why not?

---

[31] John 14:15–17, 16:13.

[32] Proverbs 16:25.

13

SHORTCUTS

Whether we drive six blocks or six hundred miles, we want to find the fastest route to get to our destination. Shortcuts can be faster, but they are not always beneficial. Shortcuts often come with a trade off or *price* to be paid. Some routes might take you through dangerous neighborhoods or along long stretches without gas or rest stations.

When married couples face difficult circumstances, one or both of them might want to turn their marriage around as quickly as possible. Each person might have their own perception of what constitutes *restoration* in their marriage. For some, if they are not arguing, everything is great. Others might believe being intimate is a *sign* that all is well.

Each time I realized how bad my marriage was, I wanted to fix it right away. I wanted to settle every argument, complaint, and problem so we could start anew. I tried to *behave* myself by not arguing, hoping my actions would be good enough to restore our marriage. But each time I resorted to this, I became disappointed when things did not work out as time went on. I did not understand that it was going to take a lot more than keeping my mouth shut, buying gifts, and taking vacations to restore our marriage. I was missing two important things:

1. Repentance. To repent is to think differently or to reconsider. It is a change in the thinking of our current state, status, and conduct. The goal for repentance should not be as a revolving door, where we *repent-sin-repent-sin*. We should want to turn from sin and not look back again.

2. Forgiveness. To forgive is to forsake, lay aside, leave, omit, put (send) away, or remit. Forgiveness is a three-way street: to forgive your offender and ask for forgiveness from those you offended and from God.

When you forgive another person, you are choosing to lay aside your feelings and desires for revenge or justice. It is treating him or her as if he or she never wronged you. This is the litmus test to determine whether you have forgiven your offender. If you are unable to treat him or her exactly the way you treated him or her before the offense occurred, you are still holding onto unforgiveness.

Many people live with their spouses for years without forgiving them for the hurt and pain they caused. They live with the scars and pains of their past, hardening their hearts and affecting their marriage and every relationship around them.

But you do not have to continue living with your scars and pains. You can forgive. Forgiveness does not require an apology or any action on the part of the offender. You forgive because you want to be free...you want to be forgiven.

For if ye forgive men their trespasses, your heavenly Father will also forgive you: But if ye forgive not men their trespasses, neither will your Father forgive your trespasses.—Matthew 6:14–15

If you want to be forgiven of your sins, forgive others from the heart.[33] God is faithful and just to forgive you of your sins and cleanse you from all unrighteousness.[34]

You also want to ask for forgiveness from those you offended. As you consider how you might have felt toward those who offended you, someone might be feeling the same way about you. It is important that you think about the needs of others (to be free of pain and guilt) and reach out to them as well.[35]

There will be some people that will welcome your apology and forgiveness, and others will not want anything to do with you. When someone does not want to speak or interact with you, provide him or her with the space he or she needs to heal. Pray for him or her and ask God to heal his or her heart, mind, and soul—this includes your spouse. Do not try to act as if everything is alright again and ignore their pain and frustration. Pray for repentance and forgiveness to usher healing, love, and obedience to God.

_____

[33] Matthew 18:21–35.

[34] Psalm 103:8–12; Proverbs 17:9; Mark 11:25; Luke 6:32–38; 1 John 1:9.

[35] Matthew 5:22–24; Philippians 2:3–4.

Spare Time

Our instant, I-need-it-now society does not prepare us to handle the slow churning of a beautiful life and marriage before God. There are no forty-eight-hour happy marriage pills or marital implants that can give you instant results. There are no shortcuts for a healthy marriage or life before God. Cutting corners and skipping steps only creates a false sense of comfort and peace. Sooner or later, something or someone will expose those missing steps, and you will find yourself (and your marriage) back at square one again.

A marriage is made up of two independent people: two hearts, two minds, and two souls that become one. Take the time to discover the appropriate route for healing, peace, and love within your life and home.

Spend the next few weeks speaking with at least two (preferably three) mature Christian couples. Take them out to dinner or a cup of coffee. Meet in a comfortable environment that will allow everyone to speak freely. Ask your spouse to accompany you.

In your conversations, ask each couple how they built a marriage by God's design. Ask them to share at least three things that helped shape their marriage. Write a summary of your conversations.

14

GPS

The Department of Defense launched the Global Positioning System (GPS) project for the United States military in 1973.[36] It was approved for civilian use in the 1980s. GPS provides many people around the world with positioning, navigation, and timing services.[37]

A marriage is similar to GPS. Where it is not important to track or pinpoint where your spouse is at any given moment, it is important to understand your role, purpose, and mission as a husband or wife. Many couples experience problems in their relationship because one or both of them do not know or want to accept the position God has given them.

---

[36] Global Positioning System, Wikipedia, accessed August 26, 2017, https://en.wikipedia.org/wiki/Global_Positioning_System.

[37] GPS Overview, GPS.gov, accessed August 26, 2017, http://www.gps.gov/systems/gps/.

God has established clear roles and responsibilities for the husband and wife. Following are several scriptures that identify these roles and responsibilities:

Husbands

Genesis 2:18–24—*And the Lord God said, It is not good that the man should be alone; I will make him an help meet for him. And out of the ground the Lord God formed every beast of the field, and every fowl of the air; and brought them unto Adam to see what he would call them: and whatsoever Adam called every living creature, that was the name thereof. And Adam gave names to all cattle, and to the fowl of the air, and to every beast of the field; but for Adam there was not found an help meet for him. And the Lord God caused a deep sleep to fall upon Adam, and he slept: and he took one of his ribs, and closed up the flesh instead thereof; And the rib, which the Lord God had taken from man, made he a woman, and brought her unto the man. And Adam said, This is now bone of my bones, and flesh of my flesh: she shall be called Woman, because she was taken out of Man. Therefore shall a man leave his father and his mother, and shall cleave unto his wife: and they shall be one flesh.*

Proverbs 5:15–19—*Drink waters out of thine own cistern, and running waters out of thine own well. Let thy fountains be dispersed abroad, and rivers of waters in the streets. Let them be only thine own, and not strangers' with thee. Let thy fountain be blessed: and rejoice with the wife of thy youth. Let her be as the loving hind and pleasant roe; let her breasts satisfy thee at all times; and be thou ravished always with her love.*

Proverbs 13:22—*A good man leaveth an inheritance to his children's children: and the wealth of the sinner is laid up for the just.*

Proverbs 18:22—*Whoso findeth a wife findeth a good thing, and obtaineth favour of the Lord.*

Proverbs 31:10-12—*Who can find a virtuous woman? for her price is far above rubies. The heart of her husband doth safely trust in her, so that he shall have no need of spoil. She will do him good and not evil all the days of her life.*

Ecclesiastes 9:9—*Live joyfully with the wife whom thou lovest all the days of the life of thy vanity, which he hath given thee under the sun, all the days of thy vanity: for that is thy portion in this life, and in thy labour which thou takest under the sun.*

1 Corinthians 7:2-6—*Nevertheless, to avoid fornication, let every man have his own wife, and let every woman have her own husband. Let the husband render unto the wife due benevolence: and likewise also the wife unto the husband. The wife hath not power of her own body, but the husband: and likewise also the husband hath not power of his own body, but the wife. Defraud ye not one the other, except it be with consent for a time, that ye may give yourselves to fasting and prayer; and come together again, that Satan tempt you not for your incontinency. But I speak this by permission, and not of commandment.*

1 Corinthians 7:12, 14–16—*But to the rest speak I, not the Lord: If any brother hath a wife that believeth not, and she be pleased to dwell with him, let him not put her away. For the unbelieving husband is sanctified by the wife, and the unbelieving wife is sanctified by the husband: else were your children unclean; but now are they holy. But if the unbelieving depart, let him depart. A brother or a sister is not under bondage in such cases: but God hath called us to peace. For what knowest thou, O wife, whether thou shalt save thy husband? or how knowest thou, O man, whether thou shalt save thy wife?*

Ephesians 5:25–33—*Husbands, love your wives, even as Christ also loved the church, and gave himself for it; That he might sanctify and cleanse it with the washing of water by the word, That he might present it to himself a glorious church, not having spot, or wrinkle, or any such thing; but that it should be holy and without blemish. So ought men to love their wives as their own bodies. He that loveth his wife loveth himself. For no man ever yet hated his own flesh; but nourisheth and cherisheth it, even as the Lord the church: For we are members of his body, of his flesh, and of his bones. For this cause shall a man leave his father and mother, and shall be joined unto his wife, and they two shall be one flesh. This is a great mystery: but I speak concerning Christ and the church. Nevertheless let every one of you in particular so love his wife even as himself; and the wife see that she reverence her husband.*

1 Timothy 5:8—*But if any provide not for his own, and specially for those of his own house, he hath denied the faith, and is worse than an infidel.*

1 Peter 3:7—*Likewise, ye husbands, dwell with them according to knowledge, giving honour unto the wife, as unto the weaker vessel, and as being heirs together of the grace of life; that your prayers be not hindered.*

Wives

Genesis 2:18—*And the Lord God said, It is not good that the man should be alone; I will make him an help meet for him.*

Genesis 3:13–16—*And the Lord God said unto the woman, What is this that thou hast done? And the woman said, The serpent beguiled me, and I did eat. And the Lord God said unto the serpent, Because thou hast done this, thou art cursed above all cattle, and above every beast of the field; upon thy belly shalt thou go, and dust shalt thou eat all the days of thy life: And I will put enmity between thee and the woman, and between thy seed and her seed; it shall bruise thy head, and thou shalt bruise his heel. Unto the woman he said, I will greatly multiply thy sorrow and thy conception; in sorrow thou shalt bring forth children; and thy desire shall be to thy husband, and he shall rule over thee.*

Proverbs 12:4—*A virtuous woman is a crown to her husband: but she that maketh ashamed is as rottenness in his bones.*

Proverbs 14:1—*Every wise woman buildeth her house: but the foolish plucketh it down with her hands.*

Proverbs 19:13–14—*A foolish son is the calamity of his father: and the contentions of a wife are a continual dropping. House and riches are the inheritance of fathers: and a prudent wife is from the Lord.*

Proverbs 21:9—*It is better to dwell in a corner of the housetop, than with a brawling woman in a wide house.*

Proverbs 31:10–31—*Who can find a virtuous woman? for her price is far above rubies. The heart of her husband doth safely trust in her, so that he shall have no need of spoil. She will do him good and not evil all the days of her life. She seeketh wool, and flax, and worketh willingly with her hands. She is like the merchants' ships; she bringeth her food from afar. She riseth also while it is yet night, and giveth meat to her household, and a portion to her maidens. She considereth a field, and buyeth it: with the fruit of her hands she planteth a vineyard. She girdeth her loins with strength, and strengtheneth her arms. She perceiveth that her merchandise is good: her candle goeth not out by night. She layeth her hands to the spindle, and her hands hold the distaff. She stretcheth out her hand to the poor; yea, she reacheth forth her hands to the needy. She is not afraid of the snow for her household: for all her household are clothed with scarlet. She maketh herself coverings of tapestry; her clothing is silk and purple. Her husband is known in the gates, when he sitteth among the elders of the land. She maketh fine linen, and selleth it; and delivereth girdles unto the merchant. Strength and honour are her clothing; and she shall rejoice in time to come. She openeth her mouth with wisdom; and in her tongue is the law of kindness. She looketh well to the ways of her household, and eateth not the bread of idleness. Her children arise up, and call her blessed; her husband also, and he praiseth her. Many daughters have done virtuously, but thou excellest them all. Favour is deceitful, and beauty is vain: but a woman that feareth the Lord, she shall be praised. Give her of the fruit of her hands; and let her own works praise her in the gates.*

1 Corinthians 13:12–16—*But to the rest speak I, not the Lord: If any brother hath a wife that believeth not, and she be pleased to dwell with him, let him not put her away. And the woman which hath an husband that believeth not, and if he be pleased to dwell with her, let her not leave him. For the unbelieving husband is sanctified by the wife, and the unbelieving wife is sanctified by the husband: else were your children unclean; but now are they holy. But if the unbelieving depart, let him depart. A brother or a sister is not under bondage in such cases: but God hath called us to peace. For what knowest thou, O wife, whether thou shalt save thy husband? or how knowest thou, O man, whether thou shalt save thy wife?*

Ephesians 5:22–24—*Wives, submit yourselves unto your own husbands, as unto the Lord. For the husband is the head of the wife, even as Christ is the head of the church: and he is the saviour of the body. Therefore as the church is subject unto Christ, so let the wives be to their own husbands in every thing.*

1 Peter 3:1–6—*Likewise, ye wives, be in subjection to your own husbands; that, if any obey not the word, they also may without the word be won by the conversation of the wives; While they behold your chaste conversation coupled with fear. Whose adorning let it not be that outward adorning of plaiting the hair, and of wearing of gold, or of putting on of apparel; But let it be the hidden man of the heart, in that which is not corruptible, even the ornament of a meek and quiet spirit, which is in the sight of God of great price. For after*

this manner in the old time the holy women also, who trusted in God, adorned themselves, being in subjection unto their own husbands: Even as Sara obeyed Abraham, calling him lord: whose daughters ye are, as long as ye do well, and are not afraid with any amazement.

As the husband is the head of his wife, he is to love her as Christ loved the church. He is to dwell with her according to knowledge, wash her with God's word, and live joyfully with her. He is not to lord over her or treat her as his slave.[38] He is to serve her as Christ served and ministered. He is to provide for his entire household.

A wife is a help meet to her husband. She will be her husband's good thing and represent his favor from the Lord. She will be her husband's crown and virtuous woman. She will submit to her husband in everything. She will be industrious, productive, and entrepreneurial, building and establishing her house to the honor and praise of those around them. She will allow the inward adorning of a meek and quiet spirit to be her apparel, which is of great price in God's sight.

We position ourselves to love and serve one another so we can remain in the proper position to serve God and fulfill His purpose. A marriage is a not fifty-fifty split or husband vs. wife. There will be days when it is 70/30 or even seem like 110/-10. There are things she is better at, and there are things I am better at. It is how God made us. And because He placed us together, we do not lack anything. We are one flesh.

---

[38] Matthew 20:25–28.

Spare Time

Share your initial thoughts after reading the scriptures for both the husband and wife.

Have you had issues accepting and/or fulfilling the roles and responsibilities the Bible establishes for husbands and wives? If so, please explain why.

What is the task, assignment, or mission that was given to your family? How are you both supporting this purpose?

If you have been out of position, how have your actions affected your life, marriage, and purpose?

If you have been unwilling to accept the roles and responsibilities outlined for you in the Bible, please spend some time in prayer and speak to other mature believers and couples about your concerns.

Name at least three ways you can provide greater love and support to your spouse.

15

MR. & MRS.
ACCEPTANCE

The first time I bought a car from a dealership was in Japan. Unlike cars in the United States, you can find an excellent used car for about three thousand dollars. For many military members, this was the most they would spend on a car. It was the most I ever spent on a car as well.

I knew very little about warranties. For many of the used vehicles I liked and test drove, there was a sign on the window describing the warranty. Some cars carried a limited warranty of six months on certain repairs. Then other cars had an *As Is-No Warranty* sign. This sign states that the seller would not be responsible for any repairs after purchase, regardless of any oral statements made about the vehicle.

Since there were no websites in 1995 to retrieve vehicle history reports, many of us took someone with us who was knowledgeable about cars to inspect the vehicle we wanted to buy. We wanted to ensure we knew the condition of the car before buying it. Though being married is not like buying a car, there are two things we can learn from this process.

1. We must know our spouses. Many of us know very little about our spouses.

Do you know your spouse's favorite color, song, television show, or meal?

Do you know what is important to your spouse and why?

Does your spouse have an issue with trusting people?

What makes your spouse happy? Sad? Does he or she get upset easily? And if so, why?

Is your spouse financially sound?

Is this your spouse's first marriage? Does he or she have children from a previous relationship? If so, what do you know about the previous relationship and how it might impact your relationship now?

How does your spouse believe children should be raised?

Before I married Tonya, I never considered questions like these. Though it would not have changed my decision to get married, it would have helped me understand who she was and how I could best love, compliment, and accept her.

God placed a desire in my heart to learn more about Tonya. As I contemplated the questions above, I realized that I could not answer them fully. I knew some things about her, but not nearly as much as I should have.

God directed me to find out what Tonya likes to do and how she spends a majority of her free time. After watching her for about a week, I discovered she enjoyed watching soap operas and a television network dedicated to women's issues.

Next, God told me to enter and coexist in her environment. Though I did not watch a lot of television at the time, each day after work, I watched television with her. And to coexist in her domestic environment, I had to learn about her shows and its plots and characters. I could not sit down ready to turn to the sports channel at the first commercial. I had to take it all in.

It took some time, but soon I knew each of the characters on the soap operas. I even started watching her shows when she was not around and giving her details on what she missed. I was enjoying her shows, and we were enjoying one another's company.

Our conversations about the shows would branch off into different topics. Plus, our conversations were not as defensive (or destructive) as in the past. Her environment became a neutral place for us to talk, learn more about one another, and grow as soul mates.

2. You must accept your spouse. Regardless of what you know about your spouse, you must accept him or her...*as is*. Just as the signs on some cars read *As Is-No Warranty*, the same goes for your spouse.

Many of us become dissatisfied and frustrated when our spouse does not perform to our expectations. But God explained to me that I have to accept Tonya as she was. It was not my place to give her ultimatums, demands, or my personal standards. It was not my job to *fix* her either. My *job* is to love and pray for her. If there are legitimate issues that affect her life and relationship with God, then there is a way to address those issues.[39] My role as her husband and brother in Christ is to help her live for God.

And it was only then that I realized I was getting in God's way. I had to be in my rightful *position* so she could blossom and grow. My expectations, ultimatums, and standards were a distraction to Tonya's growth in Christ.

To accept her, I had to understand her and dwell with her according to knowledge.[40] She is from the east coast, and I am from the west. We were raised entirely different and had different experiences that shaped our lives before we met. How I approach a particular issue is often quite different from how she would approach it. Her way is not wrong because it is not how I would have handled it, just like my way might not be wrong. We each have differences of opinion and thought. If we both thought alike, we would have the same blind spots and problems.

I had to understand that God did not put us together by accident. We are unique people who were intentionally brought together for a specific purpose. She is right for me, and I am right for her. And I must accept her for who she is.

---

[39] Galatians 6:1–2; Hebrews 10:22–25.

[40] 1 Peter 3:7.

Tonya is the woman I need in my life. God decided this from the beginning of time. She is my good thing, and I will accept her...*as is*.

Spare Time

It is important that you know your spouse and accept him or her for who he or she is, quirks and all. Loving your spouse is not based on what he or she does for you or how he or she behaves. Allow your spouse the freedom to be him or herself without the fear of retribution or complaint. Gently love and guide them toward the Father.

How well do you know your spouse? Were you able to answer the questions at the beginning of the chapter?

Have you accepted your spouse for who he or she is? Why or why not?

Has your spouse had to perform for your love and acceptance? Have you had to perform for your spouse's love and acceptance? If so, please explain how. Has this created a negative environment in your home? If so, please explain.

Ask God to show you the environment where your spouse spends a majority of his or her free time and how you can coexist in that environment (or another) with him or her.

What is your spouse's domestic environment?

What has God revealed about how you can enter and coexist in that domestic environment?

16

MEDICINE
OF TRUTH

Ahab, the seventh king of Israel, was an evil ruler in the sight of the Lord.[41] He was married to one of the most infamous women in the Bible, Jezebel.[42] She led him into idol worship and had an evil influence over him. Ahab did more to provoke God to anger than all the kings of Israel before him.[43]

After Israel experienced three years of peace with Syria, Jehoshaphat, the king of Judah, came to Ahab. He asked Ahab if he would go to battle with him against Syria.[44] Although Ahab

---

[41] 1 Kings 16:30.

[42] 1 Kings 16:31.

[43] 1 Kings 16:33.

[44] 1 Kings 22:1–3.

initially agreed, Jehoshaphat wanted him to inquire the word of the Lord about the matter.

After Ahab gathered four hundred prophets, they each said, *Go up; for the Lord shall deliver it into the hand of the king.* But even after hearing four hundred prophets, Jehoshaphat asked if there was another prophet they could speak to.[45]

There was one additional prophet, but Ahab hated him because he never had any good prophecies about him, only evil ones. So as Ahab had Micaiah summoned, all the prophets continued to say, *Go up to Ramoth-gilead and triumph; the Lord will give it into the hand of the king.*[46]

When Micaiah came before them, he told Ahab that he saw all Israel scattered on the mountains, like sheep with no master. He declared that the Lord sent a lying spirit to speak through the four hundred prophets to entice him into battle. But he would not be successful, for the Lord declared disaster for him.

Many of us are like Ahab, wanting to hear only good things and not evil. As a prophet, Micaiah would have shared the words of God to correct Ahab's behavior and return him to God. But Ahab considered Michaiah's words evil for him because it was not what he wanted to hear.

Though he learned from Micaiah that four hundred prophets lied about his success in battle, he proceeded anyway. He did not want to listen to the one voice among four hundred. And for his refusal to hear to Micaiah, he lost his life in the battle.[47]

---

[45] 1 Kings 22:7.

[46] 1 Kings 22:12.

[47] 1 Kings 22:29–40.

A true witness delivereth souls: but a deceitful witness speaketh lies.—Proverbs 14:25

Outside of God, there might be no greater witness in our lives than our spouses. Our spouses see what many of our friends, family, co-workers, and associates might never see. They see us as we truly are. But like Ahab, we might not want to hear the truth.

How often do we fight with our spouses (and others) to protect the image we have of ourselves? Though we know they are speaking the truth about our actions, we do not want to accept the bitter truth of who we are. We would rather fight to maintain our false self-image.

Faithful are the wounds of a friend; but the kisses of an enemy are deceitful.—Proverbs 27:6

The truth can be very painful to accept. But God told me that I needed to discover the truth of who I was before any change could occur in my life. There could be no sugar coating, hiding, or dodging the truth. I had to know the *real* Hamp Lee III, not who I thought I was or desired to be.

I knew my true witness was Tonya. She is very discerning and brutally honest about the character of others. There is no sugarcoating, hiding, or dodging with her. In the past, I could not handle the level of honesty she used to describe my behavior or character. Instead of being quick to listen, slow to speak, and slow to become angry,[48] I would immediately become angry and fight to defend my reputation and false self-image. I was more interested in

---

[48] James 1:19.

maintaining my self-image than accepting the truth from the woman who loves me and cannot stand to see me hurt myself or our marriage.

Though I was not looking forward to Tonya telling me about myself, I knew her perspective would be beneficial. When God showed me a peaceful moment to speak with her, I asked her about the man she thought I was. (God told me to allow her to express herself and not say anything in response.)

As I listened, she depicted a man who broke her heart and tore at her soul. I could not believe I had mistreated her as I did. I cried at the realization that I was not the great husband I thought I was. I was ashamed. Though she was empowering me with the necessary tools to chisel away my negative behaviors, I wished I could have disappeared or run away. I did not want to face the man I had become. But after a few days of self-pity and guilt, I asked for God's help as I decided to face my most fearsome foe: me.

Spare Time

We all would like to think we are good, morally upright individuals. But from time-to-time, we might need to consider how our words and deeds are viewed by others. If we are not careful, we might lie to ourselves and others to escape the bitter reality of our true character. Though some of us need to overhaul our conduct, the prospect of restoration is not out of reach. Remember, nothing is impossible with God.[49]

---

[49] Matthew 19:26.

The path to restoration in your life and marriage begins with an honest look at who you are. There are many things you might be able to identify within yourself. But outside of God, your spouse can often provide the greatest insight into the person you do not see (or want to see) within.

Pray for a time when you might be able to speak to your spouse about the type of person you are without arguing or reprisal. God will reveal a perfect time to talk to your spouse. You do not have to rush anything, and it may not happen in one sitting.

Please listen to what your spouse is saying without thinking about any retaliating remarks or comments. Do not listen long enough to prepare a swift comeback and block out everything else your spouse is saying. Listen more than you speak.

During the conversation, ask questions that will help you understand your spouse's point of view. Allow him or her to voice his or her opinion, without your negative comments or facial expressions. You want to find out how your spouse sees you, not helping your spouse understand your point of view.

A gentle answer turns away wrath, but a harsh word stirs up anger.—Proverbs 15:1

When the conversation is over, thank your spouse for his or her honesty. Write a summary of your conversation, whether you agree with what was said or not. Please understand that your spouse is sharing his or her perception of you. Pray about what was shared.

The areas you might be lacking in can be learned and developed. It might take some time, but with God's help (and others), you can become the person He has purposed you to be. Do not allow the guilt of who you were to affect who you can become for God and your spouse.[50]

Do not be like Ahab. Allow the bitter truth to heal your soul. Humble yourself so that God might lift you up.[51]

---

[50] 1 John 3:18–20.

[51] Proverbs 16:18; James 4:10; 1 Peter 5:6.

17

THE GREAT
PURSUIT

Recently, a friend asked me what would make me happy in life. When you consider what might make you happy, you could think of all the things you ever wanted. But without hesitation, I answered, *Nothing. Nothing would make me happy.*

Throughout my life, I have seen a lot of great things, been to a lot of great places, served in great positions, and owned many things. But none of it was enough. Before I could finish celebrating and enjoying what I received, I was off to the next adventure and goal. My life was one giant checklist that I could never complete.

In the book of Ecclesiastes, the Preacher, King Solomon of Israel, was on a pursuit of his own. As his riches and wisdom exceeded any of the kings on the earth,[52] he withheld nothing from

---

[52] 1 Kings 10:23.

his heart and life.[53] Like many of us, he used his wealth and position to experience all that life had to offer. But he came to learn that many things in life were vanity. Below are ten of his assessments about the vanity of life:

1. Everything is vanity, including all the works that are done under the sun, which are grievous.[54]

2. Allowing your heart to be tested and enjoy pleasure.[55]

3. There is no remembrance of the wise more than the fool forever. The days will come when both are forgotten, as the wise dies just like the fool.[56]

5. All your toil will be left to someone who comes after you, and you do not know whether he or she will be wise or a fool. Yet, he or she will be master of all you toiled over and will enjoy it for themselves (who did not toil for it).[57]

6. Days are full of sorrow and work is a vexation. Even in the night, your heart does not rest.[58]

---

[53] Ecclesiastes 2:1.

[54] Ecclesiastes 1:1–2, 14, 2:11, 17.

[55] Ecclesiastes 2:1.

[56] Ecclesiastes 2:15–16, 3:19.

[57] Ecclesiastes 2:18–19, 6:2.

[58] Ecclesiastes 2:23.

7. The one who pleases God will receive wisdom, knowledge, and joy, but the sinner will receive travail (gathering and collecting) that he might give it to him who pleases God.[59]

8. Work and skill in work come from a man's envy of his neighbor.[60]

9. A man's eyes are never satisfied with riches. He never asks, *For whom do I labour, and bereave my soul of good?*[61]

10. If you should live many years, rejoice in them all, but remember there will be many days of darkness.[62]

The wealthiest and wisest man experienced many of the things we go after (and want to experience) on a daily basis. Many people want status, wealth, and health, and often sacrifice many things to get it, including their families. But in all Solomon experienced, he shared two important messages.

The first is from Ecclesiastes 12:13: *Let us hear the conclusion of the whole matter: Fear God, and keep his commandments: for this is the whole duty of man.*

It is the whole duty of man to fear God and keep His commandments. Solomon considers this as is your responsibility above all else. The fear of God is the beginning of wisdom.[63] Our

---

[59] Ecclesiastes 2:26.

[60] Ecclesiastes 4:4.

[61] Ecclesiastes 4:7–8, 5:10.

[62] Ecclesiastes 11:7–9.

[63] Proverbs 9:10.

fear would drive us to learn, experience, and keep His ways. The fear of God leads to life, satisfaction, and confidence in Him.[64]

The second message from Solomon fits within our discussion of marriage:

Live joyfully with the wife whom thou lovest all the days of the life of thy vanity, which he hath given thee under the sun, all the days of thy vanity: for that is thy portion in this life, and in thy labour which thou takest under the sun.—Ecclesiastes 9:9

Joyfully is described as an experience of enjoyment that encompasses how we think, what we see, and how we perceive. These experiences should guide our days with our spouses. Each day is a gift and is not promised to us. And I believe we would do well to make the most of each moment we have with our spouses. But as I described, many of us might not see our marriages or spouses as something and someone to enjoy.

Long after many of us check our *marriage box*, we are off to be well-known, well-liked, and be the very best in our profession. Many of us obsess over it day and night. But all the while, we forget to live joyfully with the person who was with us in our days of small beginnings. They stood by us when few people did, hoping we would notice them. But we only see them as an accessory or a *tool*. We no longer see the beauty, importance, or love they bring to our lives.

---

[64] Proverbs 10:27, 14:26–27, 19:23.

Bronnie Ware, once a palliative care nurse, shared five common regrets from her patients.[65] She said almost all of her patients were more concerned with their relationships than money, fame, or success. One of the top five regrets was wishing they did not work so hard. Ware said every male patient had this regret. They wished they had spent more quality time with their families. They missed their children growing up and did not spend enough time with their spouses.

I am sad and ashamed that each day of our twenty-one years together has not been joyful. I spent too many years fighting, arguing, and trying to be *somebody*. But I can change that today. Saving or pushing off enjoying my wife until tomorrow might never come. I have today. I have right now. (I stopped typing to hug and kiss Tonya; to bless her with my *magic* fingers and arms.) God gave me someone to share my life with and help complete the purpose He gave us. I can live joyfully with her now.

God gave you someone to share your life with and help complete the purpose He gave you. Enjoy him. Enjoy her. Laugh. Take photos. Create lasting memories of happiness, joy, and peace. Rejoice in the days you have together.

---

[65] The 5 Things People Regret Most On Their Deathbed, Business Insider, accessed August 30, 2017, http://www.businessinsider.com/5–things–people–regret–on–their–deathbed–2013–12.

(com)mission™

PUBLISHING

www.commissionpubs.com
info@commissionpubs.com

www.ingramcontent.com/pod-product-compliance
Lightning Source LLC
Chambersburg PA
CBHW071627040426
42452CB00009B/1522